County Seat Quilts

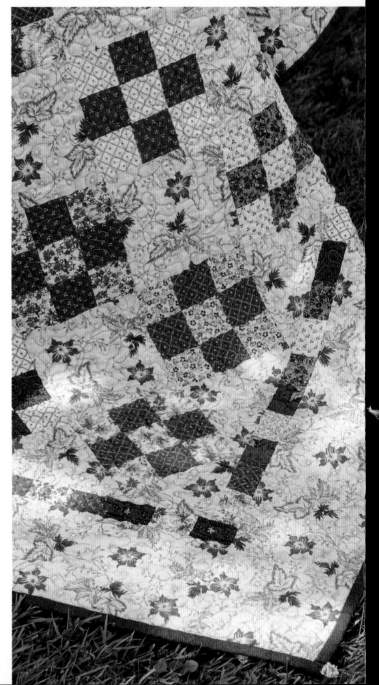

County Seat Quilts

12 Classic Patterns with Looks That Last

Julie Hendricksen and Vickie Gerike

Martingale®
Create with Confidence

County Seat Quilts: 12 Classic Patterns with Looks That Last
© 2021 by Julie Hendricksen and Vickie Gerike

Martingale®
18939 120th Ave. NE, Ste. 101
Bothell, WA 98011-9511 USA
ShopMartingale.com

Printed in Hong Kong
26 25 24 23 22 21   8 7 6 5 4 3 2 1

Library of Congress Cataloging-in-Publication Data is available upon request.

ISBN: 978-1-68356-130-9

MISSION STATEMENT

We empower makers who use fabric and yarn to make life more enjoyable.

CREDITS

PUBLISHER AND
CHIEF VISIONARY OFFICER
Jennifer Erbe Keltner

CONTENT DIRECTOR
Karen Costello Soltys

ACQUISITIONS AND
DEVELOPMENT EDITOR
Laurie Baker

TECHNICAL EDITOR
Nancy Mahoney

COPY EDITOR
Melissa Bryan

ILLUSTRATOR
Christine Erikson

DESIGN MANAGER
Adrienne Smitke

PRODUCTION MANAGER
Regina Girard

BOOK DESIGNER
Missy Shepler

COVER DESIGNER
Mia Mar

PHOTOGRAPHERS
Adam Albright
Brent Kane

SPECIAL THANKS
*Photography for this book was taken at the home of
Lianne Anderson of Arlington, Washington.*

Contents

Introduction

As the owner of J.J. Stitches quilt shop in Sun Prairie, Wisconsin, I'm always looking for new ideas to showcase fabrics and quilt patterns in ways that will captivate my customers. I like to give shoppers reasons to come back and visit the shop regularly. Recently I did this by introducing everyone to what we called the Red Chair Club. Every month over the course of a year, we featured a new quilt pattern, draped on a table in our shop along with a little red chair from the Appleton Toy and Furniture Company located in Appleton, Wisconsin. The little chair certainly stood out and became a fun feature for customers to look for whenever they came in the shop. Each month, shoppers would discover a new quilt pattern designed by Vickie Gerike, who also works at the shop.

Now you, too, can be part of the club, with a year's worth of easy lap-quilt patterns. As you can see from the photos, the quilts work equally well on a table, draped on your favorite chair or sofa, or as decorative fabric art displayed on a wall. All of the patterns are easy to stitch; many don't have a single triangle in sight! Vickie stitched all of the quilts in reproduction fabrics (my shop's specialty) and they all feature red fabrics—a color both Vickie and I love. (After all, they were for our *Red* Chair Club!) But of course, you can switch up the color scheme to showcase your favorite colors and prints.

The mornings flew by as we planned a new quilt for the next month. While you may not be inclined to stitch all 12 patterns, each one is certainly easy enough to complete in a month. We hope you love the patterns as much as we do, and we hope you can find a little red chair (or a chair of any color) to hold your quilts as your collection grows.

Julie Hendricksen

Autumn

Mixing and matching the lovely shades of fall makes stitching the quilt sheer joy. Each block is made of four Nine Patches—matching or not. Make the blocks as scrappy as you like to put your personal stamp on Autumn.

FINISHED SIZE: 54" × 54" ▪ FINISHED BLOCK: 4½" × 4½"

Materials

Yardage is based on 42"-wide fabric. Fat eighths measure 9" × 21".

20 fat eighths of assorted prints in blue, red, cheddar, green, gold, and brown for blocks

⅞ yard of cream print for setting squares

1⅞ yards of red print for setting triangles, border, and binding

3⅜ yards of fabric for backing

60" × 60" piece of batting

Cutting

All measurements include ¼" seam allowances.

From *each* of the assorted prints, cut:
    6 strips, 1¼" × 21" (120 total)

From the cream print, cut:
    5 strips, 5" × 42"; crosscut into 36 squares, 5" × 5"

From the red print, cut:
    2 strips, 8" × 42"; crosscut into:
    ▪ 6 squares, 8" × 8"; cut the squares into quarters diagonally to yield 24 side triangles
    ▪ 2 squares, 5" × 5"; cut the squares in half diagonally to yield 4 corner triangles
    6 strips, 5" × 42"
    6 strips, 2¼" × 42"

Designed, pieced, and quilted by Vicki Gerike

Making the Blocks

Sort your print strips into 10 pairs. Each pair will have six strips of one color and six of a contrasting color. Starting with one pairing, follow steps 1–5, then repeat for each additional pairing. In the featured quilt, most of the blocks are composed of one light and one dark fabric, but a few blocks are constructed using a pairing of two darks. Press seam allowances in the directions indicated by the arrows.

1 Using one set of strips, sew a dark strip to each long side of a light strip to make a strip set. Make two strip sets measuring 2¾" × 21", including seam allowances. Crosscut the strip sets into 30 segments, 1¼" × 2¾". Repeat to make a total of 10 sets of 30 matching segments (300 total).

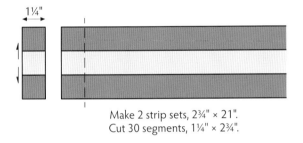

Make 2 strip sets, 2¾" × 21".
Cut 30 segments, 1¼" × 2¾".

2 Using the same fabric pairing as in step 1, sew a light strip to each long side of a dark strip to make a strip set. Make two strip sets measuring 2¾" × 21", including seam allowances. Crosscut the strip sets into 30 segments, 1¼" × 2¾". Repeat to make a total of 10 sets of 30 matching segments (300 total).

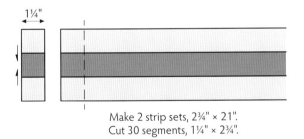

Make 2 strip sets, 2¾" × 21".
Cut 30 segments, 1¼" × 2¾".

3 Using segments from the same two fabrics, join two segments with two dark squares and one segment with one dark square to make an A unit measuring 2¾" square, including seam allowances. Make five matching units (100 total).

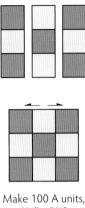

Make 100 A units,
2¾" × 2¾".

4 Using segments from the same set of strips, join two segments with two light squares and one segment with one light square to make a B unit measuring 2¾" square, including seam allowances. Make five matching units (100 total).

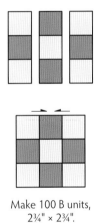

Make 100 B units,
2¾" × 2¾".

5 Lay out two matching A units and two matching B units in two rows of two units each. Sew the units into rows. Join the rows to make a block measuring

5" square, including seam allowances. Make 49 blocks. You'll have two A and two B units left over.

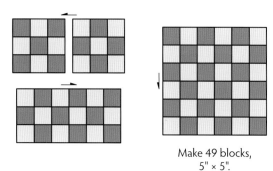

Make 49 blocks, 5" × 5".

In most of the blocks, the A and B units contain the same two fabrics. To add interest, however, some of the blocks use A and B units from two different fabric combinations.

Assembling the Quilt Top

1 Lay out the blocks, cream squares, and red side triangles in 13 diagonal rows as shown in the quilt assembly diagram. Sew the pieces into rows. Join the rows, and then add the red corner triangles.

Quilt assembly

2 Trim and square up the quilt top, making sure to leave ¼" beyond the points of all blocks for seam allowances. The quilt top should measure 45" square, including seam allowances.

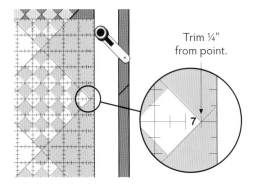

Trim ¼"
from point.

3 Join the red 5"-wide strips end to end. From the pieced strip, cut two 45"-long strips and two 54"-long strips. Sew the shorter strips to opposite sides of the quilt top. Sew the longer strips to the top and bottom edges. Press the seam allowances toward the border strips. The quilt top should measure 54" square.

Finishing the Quilt

For more details on any finishing steps, visit ShopMartingale.com/HowtoQuilt for free downloadable information.

1 Layer the quilt top with batting and backing; baste the layers together.

2 Quilt by hand or machine. The quilt shown is machine quilted with an allover meandering design.

3 Use the red 2¼"-wide strips to make binding and then attach the binding to the quilt.

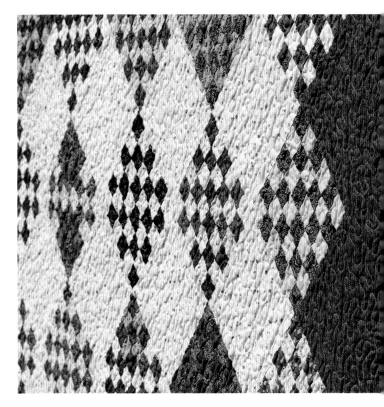

Betsy

Create an homage to Betsy Ross that couldn't be easier.
Choose red checks or stripes for simple three-piece flag blocks,
and you'll be finished with this patriotic beauty in no time.

FINISHED SIZE: 63½" × 63½" ■ FINISHED BLOCKS: 6" × 6" and 4½" × 4½"

Materials

Yardage is based on 42"-wide fabric. Fat quarters measure 18" × 21".

⅓ yard *each* of 5 assorted red checks and stripes for Flag blocks

⅓ yard of blue print A for Flag and Ohio Star blocks

1 fat quarter of blue print B for Flag blocks

1 fat quarter of blue print C for Flag and Ohio Star blocks

1⅝ yards of beige print for Ohio Star blocks, sashing, and inner border

1⅝ yards of red stripe for outer border*

½ yard of red check for binding

4 yards of fabric for backing

70" × 70" piece of batting

*If you're not using a stripe and don't mind piecing the outer border strips, you'll need only 1 yard of fabric.

Cutting

All measurements include ¼" seam allowances.

From *each* of the assorted red checks and stripes, cut:
  3 strips, 3½" × 42"; crosscut into:
   - 10 squares, 3½" × 3½" (50 total; 2 are extra)
   - 10 rectangles, 3½" × 6½" (50 total; 2 are extra)

From blue print A, cut:
  2 strips, 3½" × 42"; crosscut into:
   - 16 squares, 3½" × 3½"
   - 2 squares, 3¼" × 3¼"
   - 4 squares, 2¾" × 2¾"
  1 strip, 2½" × 42"; crosscut into:
   - 4 squares, 2½" × 2½"
   - 8 squares, 2" × 2"

From blue print B, cut:
  4 strips, 3½" × 21"; crosscut into 16 squares, 3½" × 3½"

From blue print C, cut:
  4 strips, 3½" × 21"; crosscut into:
   - 16 squares, 3½" × 3½"
   - 4 squares, 2¾" × 2¾"
  1 strip, 2" × 21"; crosscut into 8 squares, 2" × 2"

Continued on page 17

Designed, pieced, and quilted by Vicki Gerike

Continued from page 14

From the beige print, cut:

3 strips, 6½" × 42"; crosscut into 42 rectangles,
2" × 6½"

1 strip, 3¼" × 42"; crosscut into:

- 2 squares, 3¼" × 3¼"
- 8 squares, 2¾" × 2¾"
- 1 square, 2½" × 2½"
- 4 squares, 2" × 2"

14 strips, 2" × 42"

From the *lengthwise* grain of the red stripe, cut:

4 strips, 5" × 54½"

From the red check, cut:

7 strips, 2¼" × 42"

Making the Flag Blocks

Press seam allowances in the directions indicated by the arrows.

Sew a red square to a blue A, B, or C 3½" square. Sew a matching red rectangle to the bottom of the two-patch unit to make a Flag block. Make 48 blocks measuring 6½" square, including seam allowances.

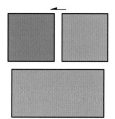 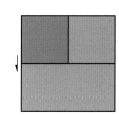

Flag block.
Make 48 blocks, 6½" × 6½".

Making the Ohio Star Blocks

1 Draw a diagonal line from corner to corner in both directions on the wrong side of the beige 3¼" squares. Layer a marked square on top of a blue A 3¼" square, right sides together. Sew ¼" from each side of *one* marked line. Cut the units apart on the unsewn marked line first, and then cut on the remaining marked line to make two triangle units and two reversed units. Repeat

using the remaining marked beige square and blue A 3¼" square to make a total of four triangle units and four reversed units.

Make 4 of each unit.

2 Join two triangle units to make an hourglass unit measuring 2½" square, including seam allowances. Make two. Join the reversed triangle units in the same manner.

Make 2 of each unit,
2½" × 2½".

3 Lay out four blue A 2½" squares, four hourglass units, and one beige 2½" square in three rows of three. Sew the pieces into rows. Join the rows to make a center Star block measuring 6½" square, including seam allowances.

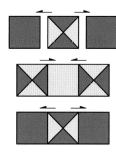 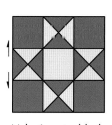

Make 1 center block,
6½" × 6½".

4 Repeat steps 1 and 2 using the beige, blue A, and blue C 2¾" squares to make 16 hourglass units measuring 2" square, including seam allowances.

5 Lay out four blue A 2" squares, four blue A hourglass units, and one beige 2" square in three rows of three. Sew the pieces into rows. Join the rows to make a block. Make two blue A corner Star blocks measuring 5" square, including seam allowances. Repeat using the blue C squares, hourglass units, and remaining beige squares to make two blue C corner Star blocks.

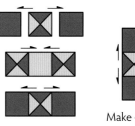

Make 4 corner blocks, 5" x 5".

Assembling the Quilt Top

1 Join seven Flag blocks and six beige 2" × 6½" rectangles to make a row. Make six rows measuring 6½" × 51½", including seam allowances.

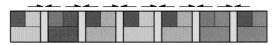

Make 6 rows, 6½" x 51½".

2 Join six Flag blocks, the center Ohio Star block, and six beige 2" × 6½" rectangles to make the center row. The row should measure 6½" × 51½", including seam allowances.

Make 1 row, 6½" x 51½".

3 Join eight beige 2"-wide strips end to end. From the pieced strip, cut six 51½"-long sashing strips.

4 Referring to the quilt assembly diagram on page 19, lay out the rows from steps 1 and 2, placing the row with the Ohio Star block in the center. Add a sashing strip between each row. Join the rows and sashing strips to make the quilt center, which should measure 51½" square, including seam allowances.

5 Join the remaining beige 2"-wide strips end to end. From the pieced strip, cut two 51½"-long strips and two 54½"-long strips. Sew the shorter strips to opposite sides of the quilt top. Sew the longer strips to the top and bottom edges. The quilt top should measure 54½" square, including seam allowances.

6 Sew red stripe 54½"-long strips to opposite sides of the quilt top. Sew a corner Ohio Star block to each end of the remaining red stripe 54½"-long strips. Sew these strips to the top and bottom edges to complete the quilt top. The quilt top should measure 63½" square.

Finishing the Quilt

For more details on any finishing steps, visit ShopMartingale.com/HowtoQuilt for free downloadable information.

1 Layer the quilt top with batting and backing; baste the layers together.

2 Quilt by hand or machine. The quilt shown is machine quilted with an allover meandering design.

3 Use the red check 2¼"-wide strips to make binding and then attach the binding to the quilt.

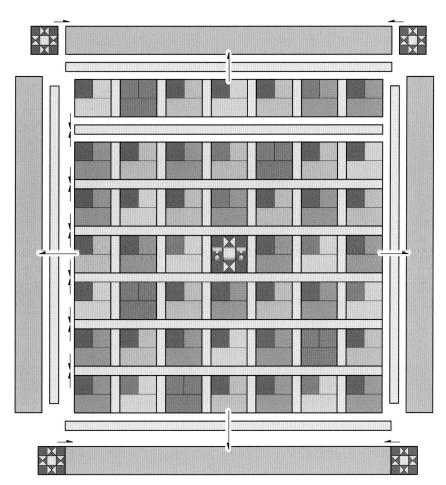

Quilt assembly

Harvest Pumpkins

Create a never-ending visit to the pumpkin patch. From the rich fall colors
to a fun twist that turns stars into pumpkins, there's plenty to love.
You'll reach for this lap quilt year after year as the temperature starts to dip.

FINISHED SIZE: 45½" × 53" ▪ FINISHED BLOCK: 6" × 7½"

Materials

*Yardage is based on 42"-wide fabric. Fat quarters measure
18" × 21"; fat eighths measure 9" × 21".*

2½ yards of brown stripe for blocks, sashing, border,
and binding

10 fat quarters of assorted prints in cream, gray, gold,
rust, and orange for blocks*

1 fat quarter *each* of gray and orange prints for blocks

1 fat eighth of brown print for pumpkin stems

3 yards of fabric for backing

52" × 59" piece of batting

**If you're shopping in your stash, you'll actually need
a 12" × 21" piece of each fabric.*

Cutting

All measurements include ¼" seam allowances.

From the brown stripe, cut:

2 strips, 8" × 42"; crosscut into 20 rectangles, 2" × 8"
3 strips, 3" × 42"; crosscut into 6 strips, 3" × 21"
4 strips, 2⅜" × 42"; crosscut into 50 squares,
    2⅜" × 2⅜". Cut the squares in half diagonally
    to yield 100 triangles.
4 strips, 2" × 36½"
5 strips, 5" × 42"
6 strips, 2¼" × 42"

From *each* of the assorted prints, cut:

4 strips, 2" × 21"; crosscut into:
  - 8 rectangles, 2" × 3½" (80 total)
  - 16 squares, 2" × 2" (160 total)
1 strip, 3½" × 21"; crosscut into:
  - 2 squares, 3½" × 3½" (20 total)
  - 4 squares, 2⅜" × 2⅜"; cut the squares in half
    diagonally to yield 8 triangles (80 total)

From the gray print, cut:

5 strips, 2" × 21"; crosscut into:
  - 8 rectangles, 2" × 3½"
  - 24 squares, 2" × 2"
1 strip, 2⅜" × 21"; crosscut into 4 squares, 2⅜" × 2⅜".
    Cut the squares in half diagonally to yield
    8 triangles.
1 strip, 3½" × 21"; crosscut into 3 squares, 3½" × 3½"

From the orange print, cut:

5 strips, 2" × 21"; crosscut into:
  - 12 rectangles, 2" × 3½"
  - 16 squares, 2" × 2"
1 strip, 2⅜" × 21"; crosscut into 6 squares, 2⅜" × 2⅜".
    Cut the squares in half diagonally to yield
    12 triangles.
1 strip, 3½" × 21"; crosscut into 2 squares, 3½" × 3½"

From the brown print, cut:

3 strips, 1½" × 21"

Making the Blocks

Pair the pieces from the 10 assorted prints into five sets of two contrasting fabrics each. For each set, label one print as A and the other print as B. Each set of A and B prints will yield two blocks with a dark pumpkin and two blocks with a light pumpkin for a total of 20 blocks. Press seam allowances in the directions indicated by the arrows.

1 Join brown stripe and A triangles to make a half-square-triangle unit. Make eight units measuring 2" square, including seam allowances. In the same way, join brown stripe and B triangles to make eight triangle units.

Make 8 of each unit,
2" × 2".

2 Draw a diagonal line from corner to corner on the wrong side of each of the A and B 2" squares. Place a marked B square on one end of an A rectangle, right sides together. Sew on the marked line. Trim the excess corner fabric, ¼" from the stitched line. Place a marked B square on the opposite end of the A rectangle. Sew and trim as before to make a flying-geese unit. Make eight A units measuring 2" × 3½", including seam allowances.

Make 8 A units,
2" × 3½".

3 Repeat step 2, using the marked A 2" squares and the B rectangles to make eight B units measuring 2" × 3½", including seam allowances.

Make 8 B units,
2" × 3½".

4 Lay out four A flying-geese units, four A triangle units, and one B 3½" square in three rows. Sew the units into rows. Join the rows to make a Star block. Make two blocks. Repeat using the B flying-geese units, B triangle units, and an A 3½" square to make two blocks. The blocks should measure 6½" square, including seam allowances.

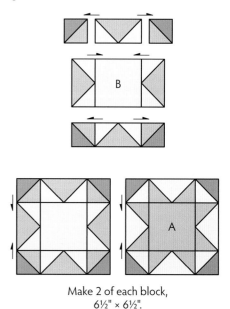

Make 2 of each block,
6½" × 6½".

5 Repeat steps 1–4 using the remaining four sets of A and B prints to make a total of 20 blocks.

Designed, pieced, and quilted by Vicki Gerike

6 Repeat steps 1–4 on page 22 using the gray and orange pieces to make two blocks with an orange star and a gray background and three blocks with a gray star and an orange background. You should now have 25 blocks measuring 6½" square, including seam allowances.

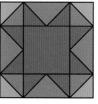 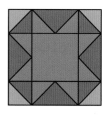

Make 2 blocks,
6½" × 6½".

Make 3 blocks,
6½" × 6½".

7 Sew a brown stripe 3" × 21" strip to each long side of a brown print strip to make a strip set measuring 6½" × 21", including seam allowances. Make three strip sets. Crosscut the strip sets into 25 segments, 2" × 6½".

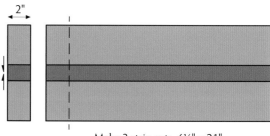

Make 3 strip sets, 6½" × 21".
Cut 25 segments, 2" × 6½".

8 Sew a segment from step 7 to the top of each Star block to make a Pumpkin block. Make 25 blocks measuring 6½" × 8", including seam allowances.

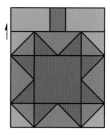

Make 25 blocks,
6½" × 8".

Assembling the Quilt Top

Refer to the photo on page 23 and the quilt assembly diagram below for placement guidance throughout.

1 Join five blocks and four brown stripe 2" × 8" rectangles to make a block row. Make five rows measuring 8" × 36½", including seam allowances.

2 Join the block rows and brown stripe 2" × 36½" strips in alternating positions to make the quilt center, which should measure 36½" × 44", including seam allowances.

3 Join the brown stripe 5"-wide strips end to end. From the pieced strip, cut two 45½"-long strips and two 44"-long strips. Sew the shorter strips to opposite sides of the quilt center. Sew the longer strips to the top and bottom edges to complete the quilt top. The quilt top should measure 45½" × 53".

Finishing the Quilt

For more details on any finishing steps, visit ShopMartingale.com/HowtoQuilt for free downloadable information.

1 Layer the quilt top with batting and backing; baste the layers together.

2 Quilt by hand or machine. The quilt shown is machine quilted with an allover meandering design.

3 Use the brown stripe 2¼"-wide strips to make binding and then attach the binding to the quilt.

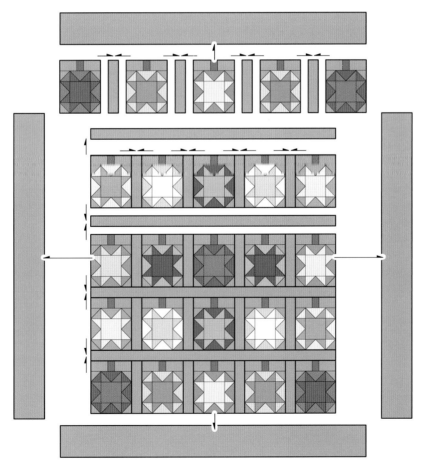

Quilt assembly

Hazel

Plus Sign quilt blocks are popular among quilters of all generations.
In Hazel, we mixed up the values of the pluses. Some are light,
some are dark, but they all add up to total scrappy fun!

FINISHED SIZE: 60½" × 60½" ■ FINISHED BLOCK: 4½" × 4½"

Materials

*Yardage is based on 42"-wide fabric. Fat eighths measure
9" × 21".*

17 fat eighths of assorted prints in beige, red, tan, and
gray for blocks

2½ yards of tan print for setting squares and triangles,
middle border, and binding

¾ yard of cream print for inner and outer borders

3¾ yards of fabric for backing

67" × 67" piece of batting

Cutting

All measurements include ¼" seam allowances.

From *each* of the assorted prints, cut:
    4 strips, 2" × 21" (68 total); crosscut *1 of the strips*
    into 4 rectangles, 2" × 5" (68 total; 4 are extra)

From the tan print, cut:
    7 strips, 5" × 42"; crosscut into 49 squares, 5" × 5"
    2 strips, 7¾" × 42"; crosscut into:
      ▪ 7 squares, 7¾" × 7¾"; cut the squares into
        quarters diagonally to yield 28 side triangles
      ▪ 2 squares, 4¼" × 4¼"; cut the squares in half
        diagonally to yield 4 corner triangles
    6 strips, 2" × 42"
    7 strips, 2¼" × 42"

From the cream print, cut:
    12 strips, 2" × 42"

Designed, pieced, and quilted by Vicki Gerike

Making the Blocks

Select two contrasting prints. Each pair of prints will make four blocks. Press seam allowances in the directions indicated by the arrows.

1 Join two strips from one print and one strip from a contrasting print to make a strip set measuring 5" × 21", including seam allowances. Crosscut the strip set into eight segments, 2" × 5".

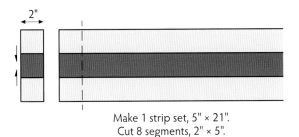

Make 1 strip set, 5" × 21".
Cut 8 segments, 2" × 5".

2 Sew a segment from step 1 to each long side of a print 2" × 5" rectangle that matches the center square in the segments. Repeat the steps to make 64 blocks measuring 5" square, including seam allowances. You'll have eight strip-set segments left over.

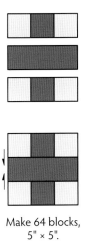

Make 64 blocks,
5" × 5".

Mixed Up and Scrappy

The early 1900s saw red-and-white Plus Sign quilts pieced, embroidered, and then raffled to support the Red Cross during World War I. We've kept the red but made our blocks scrappy, and added a few low-contrast blocks to the mix. Including several blocks that fade into the setting squares and triangles gives depth to the overall look.

Assembling the Quilt Top

When adding the cream and tan strips in steps 4–6, press the seam allowances toward each newly added border.

1 Lay out the blocks, tan 5" squares, and tan side triangles in 15 diagonal rows as shown in the quilt assembly diagram below. Sew the pieces into rows. Join the rows, and then add the tan corner triangles.

2 Trim and square up the quilt top, making sure to leave ¼" beyond the points of all blocks for seam allowances. The quilt top should measure 51½" square, including seam allowances.

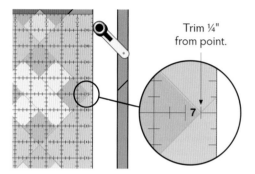

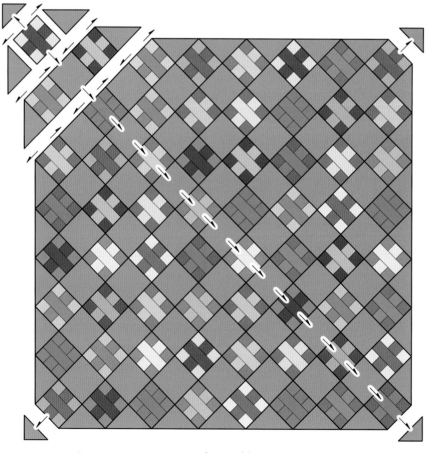

Quilt assembly

3 Join the cream 2"-wide strips end to end. From the pieced strip, cut two 60½"-long strips, two 57½"-long strips, two 54½"-long strips, and two 51½"-long strips.

4 Sew the cream 51½"-long strips to opposite sides of the quilt center. Sew the cream 54½"-long strips to the top and bottom edges. The quilt top should measure 54½" square, including seam allowances.

5 Join the tan 2"-wide strips end to end. From the pieced strip, cut two 54½"-long strips and two 57½"-long strips. Sew the shorter strips to opposite sides of the quilt center. Sew the longer strips to the top and bottom edges. The quilt top should measure 57½" square, including seam allowances.

6 Sew the cream 57½"-long strips to opposite sides of the quilt center. Sew the cream 60½"-long strips to the top and bottom edges to complete the quilt top. The quilt top should measure 60½" square.

Finishing the Quilt

For more details on any finishing steps, visit ShopMartingale.com/HowtoQuilt for free downloadable information.

1 Layer the quilt top with batting and backing; baste the layers together.

2 Quilt by hand or machine. The quilt shown is machine quilted with an allover meandering design.

3 Use the tan 2¼"-wide strips to make binding and then attach the binding to the quilt.

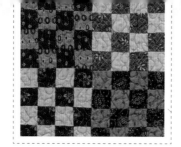

Ida Mae

Checkers, anyone? Dig through your stash, pull out your scrap bin, or head to the quilt shop to curate the perfect fabric mix for an easy-to-piece and easy-to-love beauty.

FINISHED SIZE: 53½" × 53½" ▪ FINISHED BLOCK: 4" × 4"

Materials

Yardage is based on 42"-wide fabric. Fat eighths measure 9" × 21".

34 fat eighths of assorted light, medium, and dark prints in blue, red, cheddar, green, brown, and gold for blocks and pieced middle border

1 yard of red print for inner and outer borders

½ yard of red stripe for binding

3½ yards of fabric for backing

60" × 60" piece of batting

Cutting

All measurements include ¼" seam allowances.

From *each* of the assorted prints, cut:
    5 strips, 1½" × 21" (170 total; 16 are extra)

From the red print, cut:
    5 strips, 1½" × 42"
    6 strips, 4" × 42"

From the red stripe, cut:
    6 strips, 2¼" × 42"

Making the Blocks

Press seam allowances in the directions indicated by the arrows.

1 Select two strips *each* from two contrasting prints. Join one strip from each print to make a strip set. Make two identical strip sets measuring 2½" × 21", including seam allowances. Crosscut the strip sets into 26 segments, 1½" × 2½".

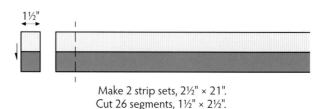

Make 2 strip sets, 2½" × 21".
Cut 26 segments, 1½" × 2½".

2 Join two segments to make a four-patch unit. Make 13 units measuring 2½" square, including seam allowances.

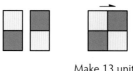

Make 13 units,
2½" × 2½".

Designed, pieced, and quilted by Vicki Gerike

3 Lay out four of the four-patch units in two rows of two units each. Sew the units into rows. Join the rows to make a 16 Patch block. Repeat the steps to make a total of 100 blocks measuring 4½" square, including seam allowances. The remaining four-patch units will be used to make the pieced border.

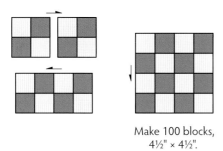

Make 100 blocks,
4½" × 4½".

Making the Four-Patch Border

1 Repeat step 1 of "Making the Blocks" on page 32 to make nine strip sets measuring 2½" × 21", including seam allowances. Crosscut each strip set into 12 segments, 1½" × 2½" (100 total).

2 Join two matching segments to make a four-patch unit. Make 54 units measuring 2½" square, including seam allowances. You will now have a total of 96 four-patch units; 88 units are needed for the pieced borders; eight will be left over, but they will give you choices as you piece the borders.

Make 54 units,
2½" × 2½".

3 Join 21 four-patch units to make a side border measuring 2½" × 42½", including seam allowances. Make two side borders.

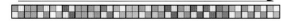

Make 2 side borders,
2½" × 42½".

4 Join 23 four-patch units to make a top border measuring 2½" × 46½", including seam allowances. Repeat to make the bottom border.

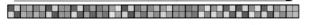

Make 2 top/bottom borders,
2½" × 46½".

Assembling the Quilt Top

1 Lay out the blocks in 10 rows of 10 blocks each as shown in the quilt assembly diagram. Sew the blocks into rows. Join the rows to make the quilt center, which should measure 40½" square, including seam allowances.

2 Join the red print 1½"-wide strips end to end. From the pieced strip, cut two 42½"-long strips and two 40½"-long strips. Sew the shorter strips to opposite sides of the quilt center. Sew the longer strips to the top and bottom edges. The quilt top should measure 42½" square, including seam allowances.

3 Sew the 42½"-long four-patch borders to opposite sides of the quilt top. Sew the 46½"-long four-patch borders to the top and bottom edges. The quilt top should measure 46½" square, including seam allowances.

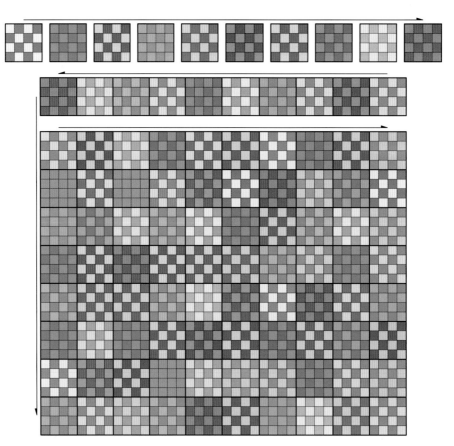

Quilt assembly

4 Join the red print 4"-wide strips end to end. From the pieced strip, cut two 46½"-long strips and two 53½"-long strips. Sew the shorter strips to opposite sides of the quilt center. Sew the longer strips to the top and bottom edges. The quilt top should measure 53½" square.

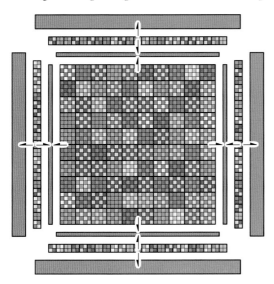

Adding borders

Finishing the Quilt

For more details on any finishing steps, visit ShopMartingale.com/HowtoQuilt for free downloadable information.

1 Layer the quilt top with batting and backing; baste the layers together.

2 Quilt by hand or machine. The quilt shown is machine quilted with an allover meandering design.

3 Use the red stripe 2¼"-wide strips to make binding and then attach the binding to the quilt.

Lucy

Stitch little Nine Patches in disguise, with the light fabrics in the corners where you'd typically find the dark prints. Be sure to choose a light print you love for the background, as the pattern really lets the fabric shine.

FINISHED SIZE: 56½" × 56½" ■ FINISHED BLOCK: 4½" × 4½"

Materials

Yardage is based on 42"-wide fabric. Fat eighths measure 9" × 21".

10 fat eighths of assorted light prints for blocks and pieced inner border

10 fat eighths of assorted dark prints in red and brown for blocks and pieced inner border

2¼ yards of beige floral for setting squares, setting triangles, and outer border

½ yard of red print for binding

3½ yards of fabric for backing

63" × 63" piece of batting

Cutting

All measurements include ¼" seam allowances.

From *each* of the assorted light prints, cut:
3 strips, 2" × 21" (30 total)

From *each* of the assorted dark prints, cut:
3 strips, 2" × 21" (30 total)

From *each of 4* dark prints, cut:
1 square, 1½" × 1½" (4 total)

From the *lengthwise* grain of the beige floral, cut:
2 strips, 5" × 56½"
2 strips, 5" × 47½"

From the remainder of the beige floral, cut:
10 strips, 5" × 21"; crosscut into 38 squares, 5" × 5". Cut *2 of the squares* in half diagonally to yield 4 corner triangles.
3 strips, 8" × 21"; crosscut into 6 squares, 8" × 8". Cut the squares into quarters diagonally to yield 24 side triangles.

From the red print, cut:
7 strips, 2¼" × 42"

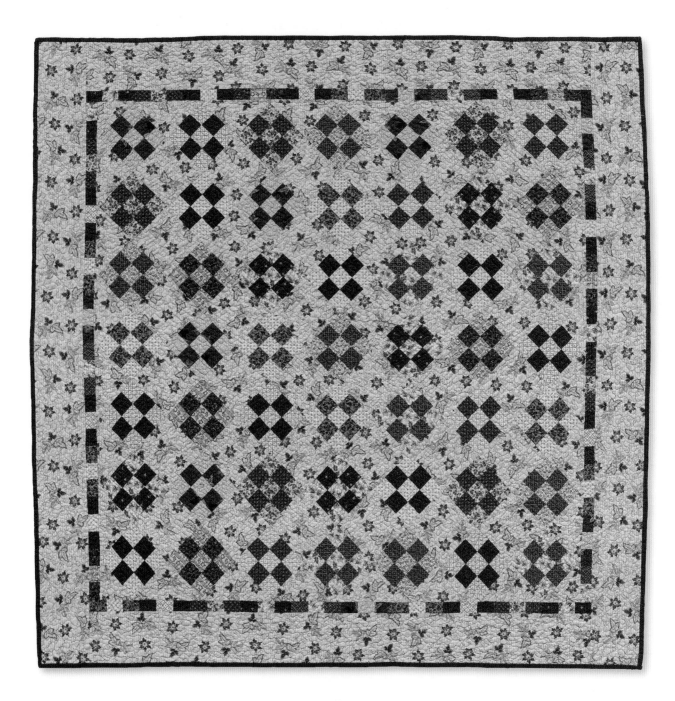

Designed, pieced, and quilted by Vicki Gerike

Making the Blocks

Sort your print strips into 10 pairs of contrasting colors. Each pair will have three matching light strips and three matching dark strips. Press seam allowances in the directions indicated by the arrows.

1 Sew matching light strips to the long sides of a dark strip to make a strip set measuring 5" × 21", including seam allowances. Make a total of 10 strip sets. Crosscut each strip set into 10 A segments, 2" × 5" (100 total).

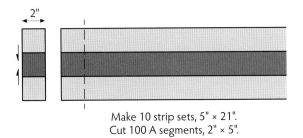

Make 10 strip sets, 5" × 21".
Cut 100 A segments, 2" × 5".

2 Using the same two prints as in step 1, sew matching dark strips to the long sides of a light strip to make a strip set measuring 5" × 21", including seam allowances. Make a total of 10 strip sets. Crosscut each strip set into five 2" × 5" B segments (50 total) and four 1½" × 5" C segments (40 total). The C segments will be used for the pieced border.

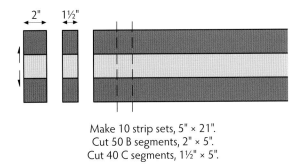

Make 10 strip sets, 5" × 21".
Cut 50 B segments, 2" × 5".
Cut 40 C segments, 1½" × 5".

3 Join two matching A segments and one B segment using the same fabrics to make a Nine Patch block. Make 50 blocks measuring 5" square, including seam allowances. You'll have one extra block to save for another project.

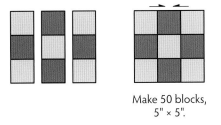

Make 50 blocks,
5" × 5".

Assembling the Quilt Top

1 Lay out the blocks, beige floral squares, and beige floral side triangles in 13 diagonal rows as shown. Sew the pieces into rows. Join the rows, and then add the beige floral corner triangles.

2 Trim and square up the quilt top, making sure to leave ½" beyond the points of all blocks for seam allowances so that the pieced border will fit correctly. The quilt top should measure 45½" square, including seam allowances.

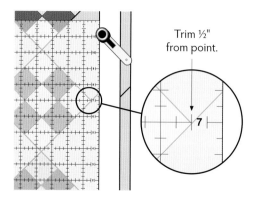

Trim ½" from point.

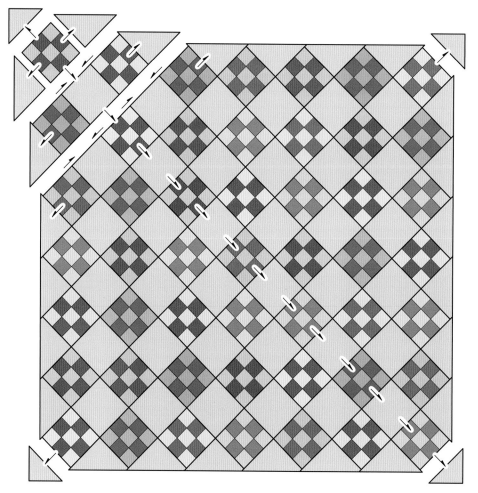

Quilt assembly

3 Join 10 C segments to make a side border measuring 1½" × 45½", including seam allowances. Make two. Make two top and bottom borders in the same manner, adding a dark square to each end. The top and bottom borders should measure 1½" × 47½", including seam allowances.

Make 2 side borders, 1½" × 45½".

Make 2 top/bottom borders, 1½" × 47½".

4 Sew the pieced borders to opposite sides of the quilt top and then to the top and bottom edges. The quilt top should now measure 47½" square, including seam allowances.

5 Sew the beige floral 5" × 47½" strips to the top and bottom edges of the quilt top. Sew the beige floral 5" × 56½" strips to opposite sides of the quilt top. The quilt top should now measure 56½" square.

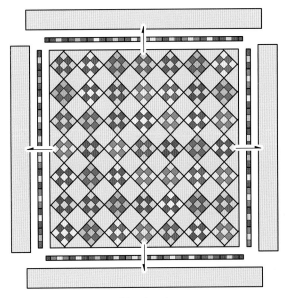

Adding borders

Finishing the Quilt

For more details on any finishing steps, visit ShopMartingale.com/HowtoQuilt for free downloadable information.

1 Layer the quilt top with batting and backing; baste the layers together.

2 Quilt by hand or machine. The quilt shown is machine quilted with an allover meandering design.

3 Use the red 2¼"-wide strips to make binding and then attach the binding to the quilt.

Miss Honey

Create a big impact from simple blocks. Basic Nine Patches
and plain squares form a dynamic crossweave design
when placed on point.

FINISHED SIZE: 54" × 65⅝"   ■   FINISHED BLOCK: 3" × 3"

Materials

*Yardage is based on 42"-wide fabric. Fat quarters measure
18" × 21".*

2 fat quarters of different beige prints for blocks

3 fat quarters of assorted red prints for blocks

1 yard of tan floral for blocks, inner border, and binding

1 yard of cream solid for blocks

1 fat quarter of tan print for blocks

3 fat quarters of assorted oat prints for blocks

2 yards of red print for setting squares, setting triangles,
    and outer border

3½ yards of fabric for backing

60" × 73" piece of batting

Cutting

All measurements include ¼" seam allowances.

From *each* of the beige prints, cut:

9 strips, 1½" × 21" (18 total)

From *each* of the assorted red prints, cut:

11 strips, 1½" × 21" (33 total)

From the tan floral, cut:

11 strips, 1½" × 42"; crosscut 5 *of the strips*
    into 10 strips, 1½" × 21" (1 is extra)
7 strips, 2¼" × 42"

From the cream solid, cut:

20 strips, 1½" × 42"; crosscut into 40 strips,
    1½" × 21". Crosscut 1 *of the strips* into 8 squares,
    1½" × 1½".

From the tan print, cut:

9 strips, 1½" × 21"

From *each* of the oat prints, cut:

11 strips, 1½" × 21" (33 total; 3 are extra)

From *each of* 2 oat prints, cut:

5 squares, 1½" × 1½" (10 total)

From the *lengthwise* grain of the red print, cut:

2 strips, 5" × 57⅝"
2 strips, 5" × 54"

From the remainder of the red print, cut:

11 strips, 3½" × 21"; crosscut into 54 squares,
    3½" × 3½"
4 strips, 5¾" × 21"; crosscut into 11 squares,
    5¾" × 5¾". Cut the squares into quarters diagonally
    to yield 44 side triangles (2 are extra).
2 squares, 5" × 5"; cut the squares in half diagonally
    to yield 4 corner triangles

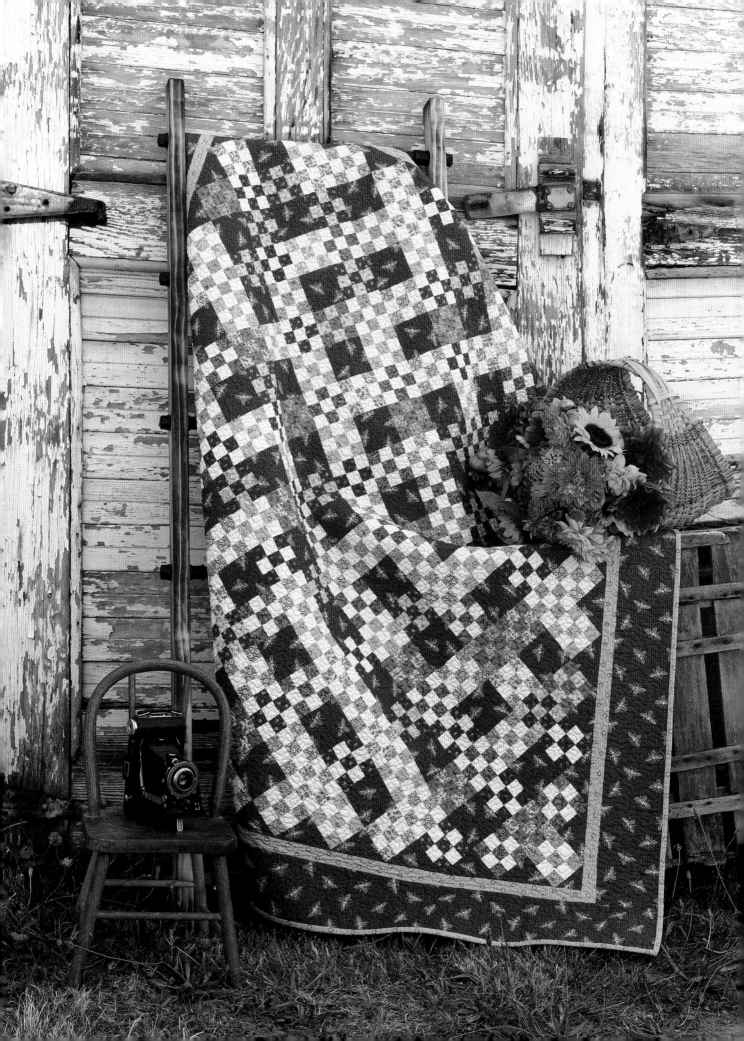

Making the A and B Blocks

Press seam allowances in the directions indicated by the arrows.

1 Sort the 1½" × 21" strips into the following combinations to make a total of 14 sets. Each set should contain three matching strips of a dark fabric and three matching strips of a light fabric.
- **Beige #1 and red.** Pair three beige and three red strips to make a set. Make three sets total, using a different red print in each set.

- **Beige #2 and red.** Using a different beige print, pair three beige and three red strips to make a set. Make three sets total, using a different red in each.

- **Tan floral and cream.** Pair three tan floral and three cream strips. Make three sets total.

- **Tan and oat.** Pair three tan print and three oat strips to make a set. Make three sets total, using a different oat print in each set.

- **Oat and cream.** Pair three oat and three cream strips to make a set. Make two sets total, using a different oat print in each set.

2 Using the strips from one set, sew a dark strip to each long side of a light strip to make a strip set measuring 3½" × 21", including seam allowances. Crosscut the strip set into 12 segments, 1½" × 3½".

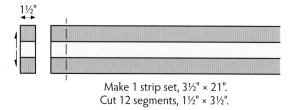

Make 1 strip set, 3½" × 21".
Cut 12 segments, 1½" × 3½".

3 Using the remaining strips from the set used in step 2, sew a light strip to each long side of a dark strip to make a strip set measuring 3½" × 21", including seam allowances. Crosscut into 12 segments, 1½" × 3½".

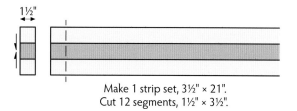

Make 1 strip set, 3½" × 21".
Cut 12 segments, 1½" × 3½".

4 Join two segments with two dark squares and one segment with one dark square to make a Nine Patch block. Make four A blocks measuring 3½" square, including seam allowances.

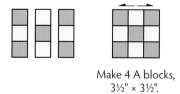

Make 4 A blocks,
3½" × 3½".

5 Join two segments with two light squares and one segment with one light square to make a Nine Patch block. Make four B blocks measuring 3½" square, including seam allowances.

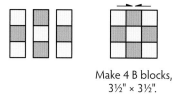

Make 4 B blocks,
3½" × 3½".

6 Repeat steps 2–5 using the remaining 13 sets of strips to make a total of 56 A blocks and 56 B blocks. Two of the B blocks will be extra.

Making the C Blocks

1 Group the remaining 1½" × 21" strips as follows.
- Five matching red and four cream strips. Make three sets total, using a different red in each set.

- Five matching oat and four cream strips. Make three sets total, using a different oat print in each set.

2 Using the red strips from one set, sew a red strip to each long side of a cream strip to make a strip set measuring 3½" × 21", including seam allowances. Make two strip sets. Crosscut into 24 segments, 1½" × 3½".

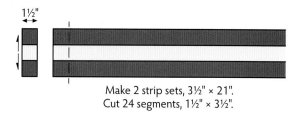

Make 2 strip sets, 3½" × 21".
Cut 24 segments, 1½" × 3½".

3 Using the remaining strips from the set used in step 2, sew a cream strip to each long side of a red

Designed, pieced, and quilted by Vicki Gerike

strip to make a strip set measuring 3½" × 21", including seam allowances. Crosscut into 12 segments, 1½" × 3½".

Make 1 strip set, 3½" × 21".
Cut 12 segments, 1½" × 3½".

4 Join two segments with two dark squares and one segment with one dark square to make a Nine Patch block. Make 12 blocks measuring 3½" square, including seam allowances. Repeat the steps using the remaining five sets of strips to make a total of 72 C blocks.

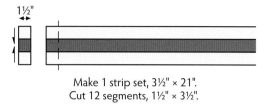

Make 72 C blocks,
3½" × 3½".

5 Join five oat and four cream squares to make a Nine Patch block. Make two C blocks measuring 3½" square, including seam allowances. You'll now have a total of 74 C blocks.

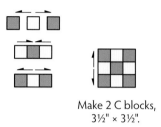

Make 2 C blocks,
3½" × 3½".

Assembling the Quilt Top

1 Lay out the A–C blocks, red 3½" squares, and red side triangles in 22 diagonal rows as shown. Even rows alternate A and/or C blocks with red squares. Odd rows alternate A and/or C blocks with B blocks. A and C blocks are used randomly throughout. Sew the blocks and red squares and triangles into rows. Join the rows, and then add the red corner triangles.

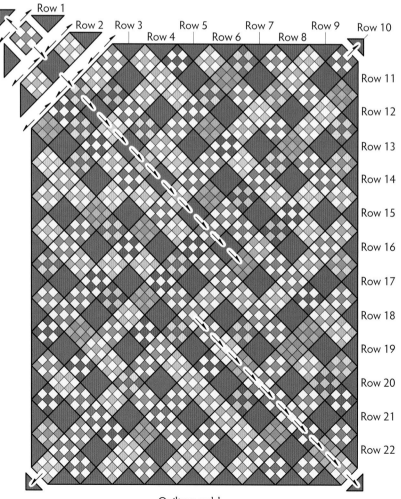

Quilt assembly

2 Trim and square up the quilt top, making sure to leave ¼" beyond the points of all blocks for seam allowances. The quilt center should measure 43" × 55⅝", including seam allowances.

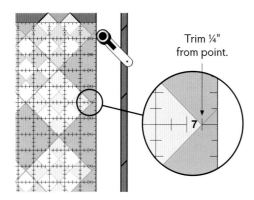

Trim ¼" from point.

3 Join the remaining tan floral 1½"-wide strips end to end. From the pieced strip, cut two 55⅝"-long strips and two 45"-long strips. Sew the longer strips to opposite sides of the quilt center. Sew the shorter strips to the top and bottom edges. Press the seam allowances toward the border. The quilt top should measure 45" × 57⅝", including seam allowances.

4 Sew the red 57⅝" strips to opposite sides of the quilt center. Sew the red 54" strips to the top and bottom edges to complete the quilt top. Press the seam allowances toward the outer border. The quilt top should measure 54" × 66⅝".

Finishing the Quilt

For more details on any finishing steps, visit ShopMartingale.com/HowtoQuilt for free downloadable information.

1 Layer the quilt top with batting and backing; baste the layers together.

2 Quilt by hand or machine. The quilt shown is machine quilted with an allover meandering design.

3 Use the tan floral 2¼"-wide strips to make binding and then attach the binding to the quilt.

Lizzie

Simple little Shoofly blocks create quite a dramatic design, especially when some have low contrast, others have lots of contrast, and some backgrounds are dark while others are light.

FINISHED SIZE: 64½" × 64½" ▪ FINISHED BLOCKS: 4½" × 4½"

Materials

Yardage is based on 42"-wide fabric. Fat quarters measure 18" × 21".

2 yards of light print for blocks

16 fat quarters of assorted dark prints in red, black, gold, and gray for blocks and pieced middle border

2 fat quarters of different beige prints for blocks

2¼ yards of gray print for setting triangles, inner and outer borders, and binding

4 yards of fabric for backing

71" × 71" piece of batting

Cutting

All measurements include ¼" seam allowances.

From the light print, cut:

25 strips, 2" × 42"; crosscut into:
- 98 rectangles, 2" × 5"
- 203 squares, 2" × 2"

5 strips, 2⅜" × 42"; crosscut into 78 squares, 2⅜" × 2⅜". Cut the squares in half diagonally to yield 156 triangles.

From *each* of the assorted dark prints, cut:

3 strips, 2" × 21"; crosscut into:
- 1 strip, 2" × 21" (16 total)
- 14 squares, 2" × 2" (224 total)

2 strips, 2⅜" × 21"; crosscut into 10 squares, 2⅜" × 2⅜" (160 total). Cut the squares in half diagonally to yield 20 triangles (320 total; 4 are extra).

From *each* of the beige prints, cut:

3 strips, 2" × 21"; crosscut into 20 squares, 2" × 2" (40 total)

2 strips, 2⅜" × 21"; crosscut into 10 squares, 2⅜" × 2⅜" (20 total). Cut the squares in half diagonally to yield 20 triangles (40 total).

From the gray print, cut:

2 strips, 8" × 42"; crosscut into:
- 7 squares, 8" × 8"; cut the squares into quarters diagonally to yield 28 side triangles
- 2 squares, 5" × 5"; cut the squares in half diagonally to yield 4 corner triangles

13 strips, 3" × 42"

7 strips, 2¼" × 42"

Designed, pieced, and quilted by Vicki Gerike

Making the Shoofly Blocks

Press seam allowances in the directions indicated by the arrows.

1 Join a light and a dark triangle to make a half-square-triangle unit. Make 39 sets of four matching units measuring 2" square, including seam allowances.

Make 39 sets of 4
matching units, 2" × 2".

2 Lay out four matching triangle units, four light squares, and one dark square in three rows of three. The dark square should match the triangle units. Sew the pieces into rows. Join the rows to make a block. Make 22 A blocks measuring 5" square, including seam allowances. You'll have 17 sets of four matching half-square-triangle units left over for step 5.

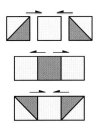

Make 22 A blocks,
5" × 5".

3 Join a beige and a dark triangle to make a half-square-triangle unit. Make 10 sets of four matching units measuring 2" square, including seam allowances.

Make 10 sets of 4
matching units, 2" × 2".

4 Lay out four triangle units from step 3, four beige squares, and one dark square in three rows of three. The dark and beige prints should be the same in all the pieces. Sew the pieces into rows. Join the rows to make a block. Make 10 B blocks measuring 5" square, including seam allowances.

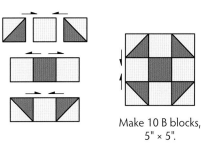

Make 10 B blocks,
5" × 5".

5 Lay out four matching triangle units from step 1, four matching dark squares, and one light square in three rows of three. The dark squares should match the triangle units. Sew the pieces into rows. Join the rows to make a block. Make 17 C blocks measuring 5" square, including seam allowances.

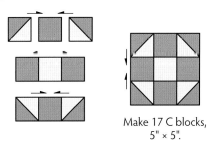

Make 17 C blocks,
5" × 5".

6 Using two different dark prints, join two dark triangles to make a half-square-triangle unit. Make 15 sets of four matching units measuring 2" square, including seam allowances.

Make 15 sets of 4
matching units, 2" × 2".

7 Lay out four matching triangle units from step 6, four dark squares that match one of the prints in the units, and one dark square that matches the other print in the units. Sew the pieces into rows. Join the rows to make a block. Make 15 D blocks measuring 5" square, including seam allowances.

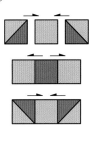

Make 15 D blocks,
5" × 5".

Making the E Blocks

Sew a light square to each side of a dark square. Sew light rectangles to the top and bottom edges to complete the block. Make 49 E blocks measuring 5" square, including seam allowances.

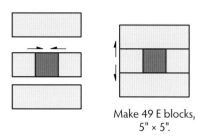

Make 49 E blocks,
5" × 5".

Assembling the Quilt Top

1 Lay out blocks A–E and the gray side triangles in 15 diagonal rows as shown in the quilt assembly diagram below. Sew the pieces into rows. Join the rows, and then add the gray corner triangles.

2 Trim and square up the quilt top, making sure to leave ¼" beyond the points of all blocks for seam allowances. The quilt top should measure 51½" square, including seam allowances.

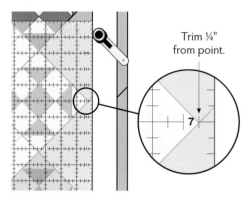

Trim ¼"
from point.

3 Join the gray 3"-wide strips end to end. From the pieced strip, cut two 64½"-long strips, two 59½"-long strips, two 56½"-long strips, and two 51½"-long strips. Sew the 51½"-long strips to opposite sides of the quilt center. Sew the 56½"-long strips to the top and bottom edges. The quilt top should measure 56½" square, including seam allowances.

Quilt assembly

4 Join the dark 2" × 21" strips end to end. From the pieced strip, cut two 59½"-long strips and two 56½"-long strips. Sew the 56½"-long strips to opposite sides of the quilt center. Sew the 59½"-long strips to the top and bottom edges. The quilt top should measure 59½" square, including seam allowances.

5 Sew the gray 59½"-long strips to opposite sides of the quilt center. Sew the gray 64½"-long strips to the top and bottom edges to complete the quilt top. The quilt top should measure 64½" square.

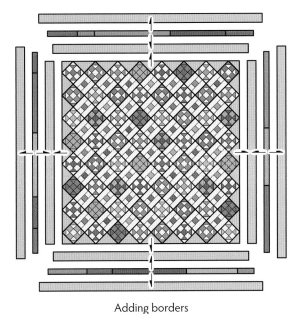

Adding borders

Finishing the Quilt

For more details on any finishing steps, visit ShopMartingale.com/HowtoQuilt for free downloadable information.

1 Layer the quilt top with batting and backing; baste the layers together.

2 Quilt by hand or machine. The quilt shown is machine quilted with an allover meandering design.

3 Use the gray 2¼"-wide strips to make binding and then attach the binding to the quilt.

Ruby

You don't have to be from Ohio to be enamored with a quilter's perennial favorite, the Ohio Star. To give this stunner the look of an antique beauty, both the blocks and the setting pieces are scrappy.

FINISHED SIZE: 48⅝" × 56" ▪ FINISHED BLOCK: 5¼" × 5¼"

Materials

Yardage is based on 42"-wide fabric. Fat quarters measure 18" × 21"; fat eighths measure 9" × 21".

8 fat eighths of assorted light prints for blocks

8 fat eighths of assorted pink, red, and brown prints (referred to collectively as "dark") for blocks

6 fat quarters of assorted brown prints for setting squares and triangles

¼ yard of red print for inner border

1⅜ yards of dark brown print for outer border and binding

3⅛ yards of fabric for backing

55" × 62" piece of batting

Cutting

From *each* of the assorted light prints, cut:

1 strip, 2¼" × 21"; crosscut into 8 squares, 2¼" × 2¼" (64 total)

2 strips, 3" × 21"; crosscut into:
- 8 squares, 3" × 3" (64 total; 4 are extra)
- 2 squares, 2¼" × 2¼" (16 total; 5 are extra)

From *each* of the assorted dark prints, cut:

1 strip, 2¼" × 21"; crosscut into 8 squares, 2¼" × 2¼" (64 total)

2 strips, 3" × 21"; crosscut into:
- 8 squares, 3" × 3" (64 total; 4 are extra)
- 2 squares, 2¼" × 2¼" (16 total; 5 are extra)

From *each* of the assorted brown prints, cut:

1 strip, 5¾" × 21"; crosscut into 3 squares, 5¾" × 5¾" (18 total)

From the remainder of the assorted brown prints, cut a *total* of:

5 squares, 9" × 9"; cut the squares into quarters diagonally to yield 20 side triangles (2 are extra)

2 squares, 5¾" × 5¾"

2 squares, 5" × 5"; cut the squares in half diagonally to yield 4 corner triangles

From the red print, cut:

5 strips, 1½" × 42"

From the dark brown print, cut:

6 strips, 5" × 42"

6 strips, 2¼" × 42"

Making the Ohio Star Blocks

Press seam allowances in the directions indicated by the arrows.

1 Draw a diagonal line from corner to corner in both directions on the wrong side of the light 3" squares. Layer a marked square on a dark 3" square, right sides together. Sew ¼" from each side of *one* marked line. Cut the units apart on the unsewn marked line first, and then cut on the remaining marked line. Make four triangle units and four reversed units.

Make 4 of each unit.

2 Repeat step 1 to make a total of 30 sets of eight matching triangle units.

3 Join two matching triangle units to make an hourglass unit measuring 2¼" square, including seam allowances. Make two. Join the reversed triangle units in the same manner.

Make 2 of each unit,
2¼" x 2¼".

4 Repeat step 3 to make 30 sets of four matching hourglass units.

5 Lay out four matching hourglass units, four dark 2¼" squares, and one light 2¼" square. The dark and light squares should match the hourglass units. Sew the pieces into rows. Join the rows to make an Ohio Star block. Make 15 blocks with dark backgrounds measuring 5¾" square, including seam allowances.

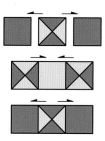 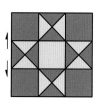

Make 15 blocks,
5¾" x 5¾".

6 Lay out four matching hourglass units, four light 2¼" squares, and one dark 2¼" square. The light and dark squares should match the hourglass units. Sew the pieces into rows. Join the rows to make a block. Make 15 blocks with light backgrounds measuring 5¾" square, including seam allowances.

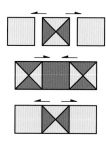 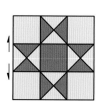

Make 15 blocks,
5¾" x 5¾".

Fabulous Florals

Do you love large-scale florals but feel they won't work in a small-sized traditional block? We set out to prove that they do work, adding large-scale florals in both the block background patches and setting squares and triangles. They certainly add interest, while the darker values in the setting pieces make the Ohio Star blocks shine.

Designed, pieced, and quilted by Vicki Gerike

Assembling the Quilt Top

1 Lay out the blocks, brown 5¾" squares, and brown side triangles in 10 diagonal rows, alternating the light and dark stars in each row as shown in the quilt assembly diagram. Sew the pieces into rows. Join the rows, and then add the brown corner triangles.

2 Trim and square up the quilt top, making sure to leave ¼" beyond the points of all blocks for seam allowances. The quilt center should measure 37⅝" × 45", including seam allowances.

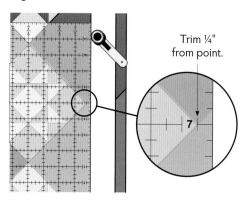

Trim ¼" from point.

Quilt assembly

3 Join the red 1½"-wide strips end to end. From the pieced strip, cut two 45"-long strips and two 39⅝"-long strips. Sew the longer strips to opposite sides of the quilt center. Sew the shorter strips to the top and bottom edges. Press the seam allowances toward the border. The quilt top should measure 39⅝" × 47", including seam allowances.

4 Join the dark brown 5"-wide strips end to end. From the pieced strip, cut two 48⅝"-long strips and two 47"-long strips. Sew the shorter strips to opposite sides of the quilt center. Sew the longer strips to the top and bottom edges. Press the seam allowances toward the outer border. The quilt top should measure 48⅝" × 56".

Finishing the Quilt

For more details on any finishing steps, visit ShopMartingale.com/HowtoQuilt for free downloadable information.

1 Layer the quilt top with batting and backing; baste the layers together.

2 Quilt by hand or machine. The quilt shown is machine quilted with an allover meandering design.

3 Use the dark brown 2¼"-wide strips to make binding and then attach the binding to the quilt.

Scarlett

Classic Sawtooth Star blocks sparkle like stars in the sky.
The secret? Make a few of the blocks with low contrast, so that
all the stars don't shine with the same degree of brightness.

FINISHED SIZE: 49½" × 58½" ■ FINISHED BLOCK: 6" × 6"

Materials

*Yardage is based on 42"-wide fabric. Fat eighths measure
9" × 21".*

10 fat eighths of assorted light prints for blocks

12 fat eighths of assorted red, gray, and tan prints
(referred to collectively as "dark") for blocks and
pieced middle border

2¾ yards of red print for setting squares, setting
triangles, inner and outer borders, and binding

3¼ yards of fabric for backing

56" × 65" piece of batting

Cutting

All measurements include ¼" seam allowances.

From *each* of the assorted light prints, cut:

1 strip, 3½" × 21"; crosscut into:
- 4 rectangles, 2" × 3½" (40 total, 4 are extra)
- 1 square, 3½" × 3½" (10 total, 2 are extra)
- 4 squares, 2" × 2" (40 total)

1 strip, 2" × 21"; crosscut into 8 squares, 2" × 2"
(80 total, 20 are extra)

1 strip, 1½" × 21"; crosscut into 7 squares, 1½" × 1½"
(70 total, 7 are extra)

From *each* of the assorted dark prints, cut:

1 strip, 3½" × 21"; crosscut into:
- 4 rectangles, 2" × 3½" (48 total, 4 are extra)
- 1 square, 3½" × 3½" (12 total)
- 4 squares, 2" × 2" (48 total)

1 strip, 2" × 21"; crosscut into 8 squares, 2" × 2"
(96 total, 4 are extra)

1 strip, 1½" × 21"; crosscut into 10 squares,
1½" × 1½" (120 total; 9 are extra)

From the red print, cut:

2 strips, 6½" × 42"; crosscut into 12 squares,
6½" × 6½"

2 strips, 10" × 42"; crosscut into:
- 4 squares, 10" × 10"; cut the squares into quarters
diagonally to yield 16 side triangles (2 are extra)
- 2 squares, 6" × 6"; cut the squares in half
diagonally to yield 4 corner triangles

3 strips, 2½" × 42"

2 strips, 2¾" × 38½"

6 strips, 5" × 42"

6 strips, 2¼" × 42"

Designed, pieced, and quilted by Vicki Gerike

Making the Sawtooth Star Blocks

For each block, you'll need eight 2" squares and one 3½" square, all matching, for the star. You'll also need four 2" squares and four 2" × 3½" rectangles, all matching, for the background. Pair your fabrics to make:

- Nine blocks with dark stars and a light background

- Eight blocks with light stars and a dark background

- Three blocks with both a dark star and a dark background

Refer to the photo on page 64 for color placement as needed. Directions are for making one block with a dark star and a light background. Press seam allowances in the directions indicated by the arrows.

1 Draw a diagonal line from corner to corner on the wrong side of eight matching dark 2" squares. Place a marked square on one end of a light rectangle, right sides together. Sew on the marked line. Trim the excess corner fabric, ¼" from the stitched line. Place a marked square on the opposite end of the light rectangle. Sew and trim as before to make a flying-geese unit that measures 2" × 3½", including seam allowances. Make four units.

Make 4 units,
2" × 3½".

2 Lay out the four flying-geese units, four light 2" squares, and one dark 3½" square in three rows of three. The light and dark squares should match the flying-geese units. Sew the pieces into rows. Join the rows to make a block. Make nine blocks measuring 6½" square, including seam allowances.

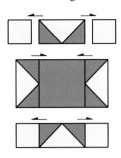 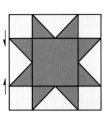

Make 9 blocks with
light backgrounds,
6½" × 6½".

3 Repeat steps 1 and 2 to make the number of blocks in the color combinations indicated below.

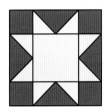 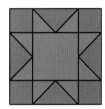

Make 8 blocks
with dark backgrounds,
6½" × 6½".

Make 3 blocks
with low contrast,
6½" × 6½".

Pieced Borders

Can't decide which color is best for the middle border when repeating the same fabric for the setting triangles and inner and outer borders? Consider adding a pieced border. Squares cut from the same fabrics you used for the blocks add just the right amount of sparkle.

Making the Pieced Border

1 Randomly join 47 light and dark 1½" squares to make a side border. Make two borders measuring 1½" × 47½", including seam allowances.

Make 2 side borders,
1½" × 47½".

2 Randomly join 40 light and dark 1½" squares to make the top border. Repeat to make the bottom border. The borders should measure 1½" × 40½", including seam allowances.

Make 2 top/bottom borders,
1½" × 40½".

Assembling the Quilt Top

1 Lay out the blocks, red 6½" squares, and red side triangles in eight diagonal rows as shown in the quilt assembly diagram below. Sew the pieces into rows. Join the rows, and then add the red corner triangles.

2 Trim and square up the quilt top, making sure to leave ¼" beyond the points of all blocks for seam allowances. The quilt top should measure 34½" × 43", including seam allowances.

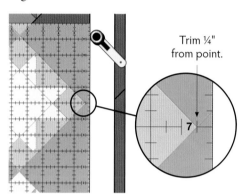

Trim ¼"
from point.

Quilt assembly

3 Join the red 2½"-wide strips end to end. From the pieced strip, cut two 43"-long strips. Sew the strips to opposite sides of the quilt center. Sew the red 2¾" × 38½" strips to the top and bottom edges. The quilt top should measure 38½" × 47½", including seam allowances.

4 Sew the 47½"-long pieced borders to opposite sides of the quilt top. Sew the 40½"-long pieced borders to the top and bottom edges. The quilt top should measure 40½" × 49½", including seam allowances.

5 Join the red 5"-wide strips end to end. From the pieced strip, cut four 49½"-long strips. Sew strips to opposite sides and then sew strips to the top and bottom edges. The quilt top should be 49½" × 58½".

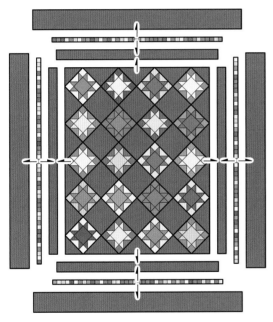

Adding borders

Finishing the Quilt

For more details on any finishing steps, visit ShopMartingale.com/HowtoQuilt for free downloadable information.

1 Layer the quilt top with batting and backing; baste the layers together.

2 Quilt by hand or machine. The quilt shown is machine quilted with an allover meandering design.

3 Use the red 2¼"-wide strips to make binding and then attach the binding to the quilt.

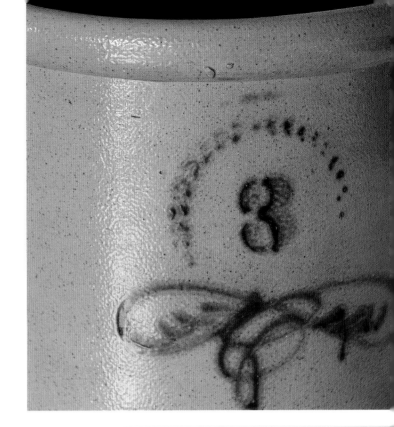

January Thaw

When the winter snows begin to melt, the changing landscape brings hope of springtime to come. Neutral fabrics create a lovely, restful palette, just like the rich earth that rests before the growing season that lies ahead.

FINISHED SIZE: 57¾" × 64½" ■ FINISHED BLOCK: 6" × 6"

Materials

Yardage is based on 42"-wide fabric. Fat quarters measure 18" × 21"; fat eighths measure 9" × 21".

15 fat eighths of assorted light prints for blocks

15 fat eighths of assorted medium and dark prints in beige and tan (referred to collectively as "dark") for blocks

6 fat quarters of assorted red prints for sashing

⅝ yard of red print for border

½ yard of red stripe for binding

3⅝ yards of fabric for backing

64" × 71" piece of batting

Cutting

From *each* of the assorted light prints, cut:
4 strips, 2" × 21" (60 total)

From *each* of the assorted dark prints, cut:
4 strips, 2" × 21" (60 total)

From *each* of the assorted red prints, cut:
1 strip, 6½" × 21"; crosscut into 11 rectangles, 1¼" × 6½" (66 total; 3 are extra)
3 strips, 1¼" × 21" (18 total)

From the remainder of 2 assorted red prints, cut a *total* of:
6 strips, 1¼" × 21"

From the red print for border, cut:
7 strips, 2½" × 42"

From the red stripe, cut:
7 strips, 2¼" × 42"

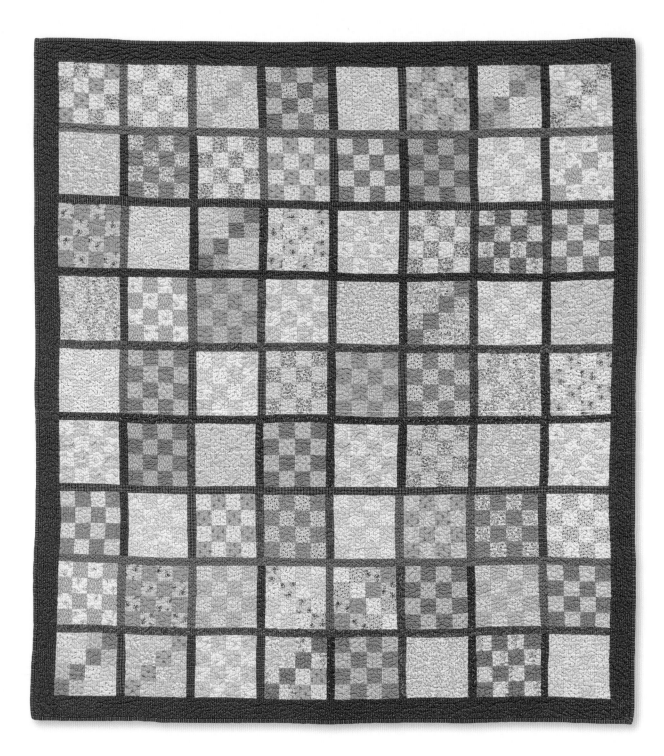

Designed, pieced, and quilted by Vicki Gerike

Making the Blocks

1 Sew a light strip to the long edge of a dark strip to make a strip set. Make two identical strip sets measuring 3½" × 21", including seam allowances. Crosscut the strip sets into 20 segments, 2" × 3½".

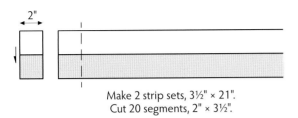

Make 2 strip sets, 3½" × 21".
Cut 20 segments, 2" × 3½".

2 Join two segments from step 1 to make a four-patch unit. Make 10 units measuring 3½" square, including seam allowances.

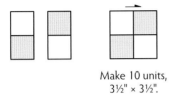

Make 10 units,
3½" × 3½".

3 Join four matching four-patch units to make a 16 Patch block. Repeat the steps to make a total of 60 blocks measuring 6½" square, including seam allowances.

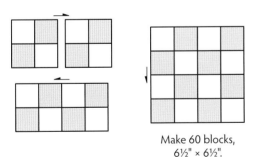

Make 60 blocks,
6½" × 6½".

4 In the same way, join two pairs of matching four-patch units to make a block. Make 12 blocks measuring 6½" square, including seam allowances.

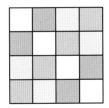

Make 12 blocks,
6½" × 6½".

Assembling the Quilt Top

1 Join eight blocks and seven red print 1¼" × 6½" rectangles to make a row. Make nine rows measuring 6½" × 53¾", including seam allowances.

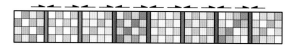

Make 9 rows, 6½" × 53¾".

2 Join three matching red print 1¼" × 21" strips end to end. Trim the pieced strip to measure 53¾" long. Repeat to make a total of eight sashing strips.

3 Lay out the rows from step 1, adding a pieced sashing strip between each row. Join the rows and sashing strips to make the quilt center, which should measure 53¾" × 60½", including seam allowances.

4 Join the red print 2½"-wide strips end to end. From the pieced strip, cut two 60½"-long strips and two 57¾"-long strips. Sew the longer strips to opposite sides of the quilt center. Sew the shorter strips to the top and bottom edges to complete the quilt top. The quilt top should measure 57¾" × 64½".

Finishing the Quilt

For more details on any finishing steps, visit ShopMartingale.com/HowtoQuilt for free downloadable information.

1 Layer the quilt top with batting and backing; baste the layers together.

2 Quilt by hand or machine. The quilt shown is machine quilted with an allover meandering design.

3 Use the red stripe 2¼"-wide strips to make binding and then attach the binding to the quilt.

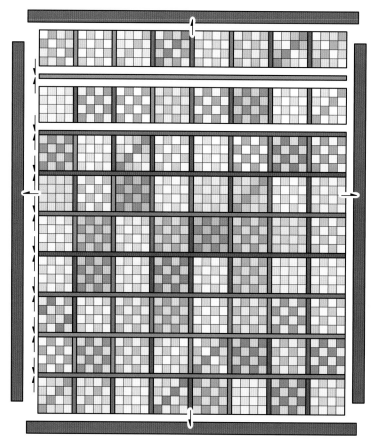

Quilt assembly

Grace

Tiny Nine Patch blocks add an element of surprise to the design. And, using them as spacers means you don't have to match triangle points from one block to the next!

FINISHED SIZE: 60¼" × 60 ¼" ■ FINISHED BLOCK: 6¾" × 6¾"

Materials

Yardage is based on 42"-wide fabric. Fat quarters measure 18" × 21"; fat eighths measure 9" × 21".

5 fat quarters of assorted green prints for A blocks*

5 fat eighths of assorted light prints for A blocks

4 fat eighths of assorted red prints for B blocks

4 fat quarters of assorted light prints for B blocks

1 fat eighth of red plaid for C blocks

1 fat eighth of light print for C blocks

1⅛ yards of light green print for C blocks and middle border

2¼ yards of red floral for setting triangles, inner and outer borders, and binding

3¾ yards of fabric for backing

67" × 67" piece of batting

If you are shopping in your stash, you'll actually need a 10" × 21" piece of each fabric.

Cutting

All measurements include ¼" seam allowances.

From *each* of the assorted green prints, cut:

    1 strip, 3⅛" × 21"; crosscut into 6 squares, 3⅛" × 3⅛"
    (30 total). Cut the squares in half diagonally to yield
    12 triangles (60 total; 8 are extra).

    2 strips, 1⅝" × 21" (10 total)

    1 strip, 2¾" × 21"; crosscut into 3 squares, 2¾" × 2¾"
    (15 total; 2 are extra)

From *each* of the light prints for A blocks, cut:

    1 strip, 3⅛" × 21"; crosscut into 6 squares, 3⅛" × 3⅛"
    (30 total). Cut the squares in half diagonally to yield
    12 triangles (60 total; 8 are extra).

    2 strips, 1⅝" × 21" (10 total)

From *each* of the assorted red prints, cut:

    1 strip, 3⅛" × 21"; crosscut into 6 squares, 3⅛" × 3⅛"
    (24 total). Cut the squares in half diagonally to yield
    12 triangles (48 total).

    2 strips, 1⅝" × 21" (8 total)

From *each* of the light prints for B blocks, cut:

    1 strip, 3⅛" × 21"; crosscut into 6 squares, 3⅛" × 3⅛"
    (24 total). Cut the squares in half diagonally to yield
    12 triangles (48 total).

    2 strips, 1⅝" × 21" (8 total)

    1 strip, 2¾" × 21"; crosscut into 3 squares, 2¾" × 2¾"
    (12 total)

From the red plaid, cut:

    5 strips, 1¼" × 21"

From the light print for C blocks, cut:

    4 strips, 1¼" × 21"

From the light green print, cut:

    9 strips, 2¾" × 42"; crosscut into:
      ▪ 32 squares, 2¾" × 2¾"
      ▪ 32 rectangles, 2¾" × 7¼"

    6 strips, 1½" × 42"

From the red floral, cut:

    2 strips, 11" × 42"; crosscut into:
      ▪ 4 squares, 11" × 11"; cut the squares into quarters
        diagonally to yield 16 side triangles
      ▪ 2 squares, 6" × 6"; cut the squares in half
        diagonally to yield 4 corner triangles

    12 strips, 3" × 42"

    7 strips, 2¼" × 42"

Making the A Blocks

Group the green and light pieces for block A into five
sets, with one green and one light print in each set.
Press seam allowances in the directions indicated by
the arrows.

1 From one set of fabrics, join a green and a light
triangle to make a half-square-triangle unit. Make 12
units measuring 2¾" square, including seam allowances.
Repeat to make 13 sets of four matching units (52 total).

Make 12 units,
2¾" × 2¾".

2 Join one green and one light strip along the long
edges to make a strip set. Make two strip sets
measuring 2¾" × 21", including seam allowances.
Crosscut the strip sets into 12 rail-fence units measuring
2¾" square, including seam allowances. Repeat to make
13 sets of four matching units (52 total).

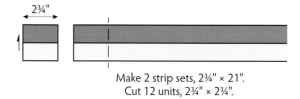

Make 2 strip sets, 2¾" × 21".
Cut 12 units, 2¾" × 2¾".

3 Lay out four triangle units, four rail-fence units,
and one green 2¾" square in three rows. The green
and light prints should be the same in all the pieces. Sew
the pieces into rows. Join the rows to make block A.
Repeat to make a total of 13 A blocks measuring 7¼"
square, including seam allowances.

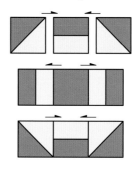 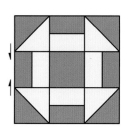

Make 13 A blocks,
7¼" × 7¼".

Making the B Blocks

Group the red and light pieces for block B into four sets, with one red and one light print in each set.

1 From one set of fabrics, join red and light triangles to make a half-square-triangle unit. Make 12 units measuring 2¾" square, including seam allowances. Repeat to make 12 sets of four matching units (48 total).

Make 12 units,
2¾" × 2¾".

2 Join one red and one light strip along the long edges to make a strip set. Make two strip sets measuring 2¾" × 21", including seam allowances. Crosscut the strip sets into 12 rail-fence units measuring 2¾" square, including seam allowances. Repeat to make 12 sets of four matching units (48 total).

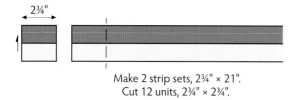

Make 2 strip sets, 2¾" × 21".
Cut 12 units, 2¾" × 2¾".

3 Lay out four triangle units, four rail-fence units, and one light 2¾" square in three rows. The red and light prints should be the same in all the pieces. Sew the pieces into rows. Join the rows to make block B. Make a total of 12 B blocks measuring 7¼" square, including seam allowances.

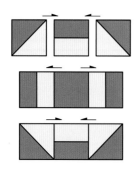 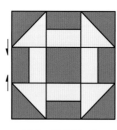

Make 12 B blocks,
7¼" × 7¼".

Making the C Blocks

1 Sew a red plaid strip to each long side of a light 1¼"-wide strip to make a strip set. Make two strip sets measuring 2¾" × 21", including seam allowances. Crosscut the strip sets into 32 segments, 1¼" × 2¾".

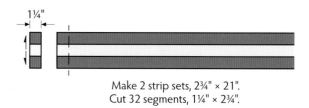

Make 2 strip sets, 2¾" × 21".
Cut 32 segments, 1¼" × 2¾".

2 Sew a light 1¼"-wide strip to each long side of a red plaid strip to make a strip set measuring 2¾" × 21", including seam allowances. Crosscut the strip set into 16 segments, 1¼" × 2¾".

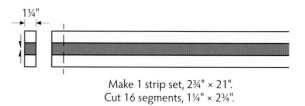

Make 1 strip set, 2¾" × 21".
Cut 16 segments, 1¼" × 2¾".

3 Join two segments with two red squares and one segment with one red square to make a nine-patch unit. Make 16 units measuring 2¾" square, including seam allowances.

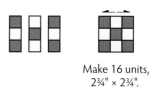

Make 16 units,
2¾" × 2¾".

4 Lay out two light green rectangles, two light green squares, and one nine-patch unit in three rows. Join the squares and unit to make the center row. Sew the rectangles to the top and bottom edges of the center row to make block C. Make 16 blocks measuring 7¼" square, including seam allowances.

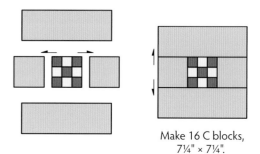

Make 16 C blocks,
7¼" × 7¼".

Designed, pieced, and quilted by Vicki Gerike

Assembling the Quilt Top

When adding the red floral and light green strips in steps 4–6 on page 79, press the seam allowances toward each newly added border.

1 Lay out blocks A–C and the red side triangles in nine diagonal rows as shown in the quilt assembly diagram below. Sew the pieces into rows. Join the rows, and then add the red corner triangles.

2 Trim and square up the quilt top, making sure to leave ¼" beyond the points of all blocks for seam allowances. The quilt top should measure 48¼" square, including seam allowances.

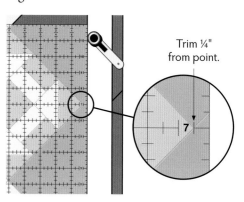

Trim ¼" from point.

Quilt assembly

3 Join the red floral 3"-wide strips end to end. From the pieced strip, cut two 60¼"-long strips, two 55¼"-long strips, two 53¼"-long strips, and two 48¼"-long strips.

4 Sew the red floral 48¼"-long strips to opposite sides of the quilt center. Sew the red floral 53¼"-long strips to the top and bottom edges. The quilt top should measure 53¼" square, including seam allowances.

5 Join the light green 1½"-wide strips end to end. From the pieced strip, cut two 55¼"-long strips and two 53¼"-long strips. Sew the shorter strips to opposite sides of the quilt top. Sew the longer strips to the top and bottom edges. The quilt top should measure 55¼" square, including seam allowances.

6 Sew the red floral 55¼"-long strips to opposite sides of the quilt top. Sew the red floral 60¼"-long strips to the top and bottom edges. The quilt top should measure 60¼" square.

Finishing the Quilt

For more details on any finishing steps, visit ShopMartingale.com/HowtoQuilt for free downloadable information.

1 Layer the quilt top with batting and backing; baste the layers together.

2 Quilt by hand or machine. The quilt shown is machine quilted with an allover meandering design.

3 Use the red floral 2¼"-wide strips to make binding and then attach the binding to the quilt.

About the Authors

Julie Hendricksen

Julie purchased her first antique quilt in 1984 and made her first quilt shortly thereafter. She has seen things change considerably in the quilting world since then. What has stayed the same, however, is her love for both vintage and reproduction scrap quilts. As an author for Martingale, a fabric designer for Windham Fabrics, and the owner of J.J. Stitches quilt shop, Julie enjoys working in an industry that continues to inspire her every day.

Julie has had such fun getting to know and work with Vickie the last couple of years. They have spent many Wednesday mornings selecting fabrics and planning quilts. They both have little red children's chairs in their homes, chairs that are now stacked with all the quilts from the Little Red Chair series!

Vickie Gerike

Vickie discovered quilting more than 30 years ago and became permanently hooked. Scrap quilts and Civil War–era designs are her favorites. She collects old quilts and antiques, and one of her treasures is her little red chair. Vickie also helps on the farm and watches her five grandkids. It's not uncommon to see her grandkids curled up on the floor with quilts. Vickie's quilts are made to be loved and used. She is inspired by the world around her, including sunsets and sunrises on the farm and the joy of seeing her grandkids growing.

Vickie has had many tough challenges, and she says that quilting has been like an old friend helping her through, along with God's grace. Working with Julie on this book has been a dream come true for Vickie because of their shared love for quilting and family.